Bad Harvest

Books by Dzvinia Orlowsky

A Handful of Bees

Edge of House

Except for One Obscene Brushstroke

Convertible Night, Flurry of Stones

Silvertone

Bad Harvest

Bad Harvest

Dzvinia Orlowsky

Carnegie Mellon University Press

Pittsburgh 2018

Acknowledgments

Grateful acknowledgment is made to the publications in which some of these poems first appeared, sometimes in different forms or with different titles:

Alembic: "Separate Bodies"; *Ashvamegh*: "Elegy," "Folding a Stranger's Laundry," "Glue Wind," "Purchasing Respirators at Home Depot for My Family, Post-2016 Election"; *The Baffler*: "Age of Osteo Collosus"; *Cardinal Points*: "Ivan the Fly Eater," "Kalendar"; *Pamplemousse*: "Mahogany Box," "Out of the Woods"; *Ploughshares*: "Fine Despite," "Pleasure Pit"; *Plume*: "Bad Harvest," "Electric Lady," "The Fortieth Day," "Given Plums," "Let the Dead Bury the Dead," "Playing Opossum," "Pussy Riot/ Want/Don't/Want," "Stone Cross," "Why I Hate Nudist Camps"; *Solstice Literary Magazine*: "Inventory," "The Weakest of Children," "Hope Was a Thing with Pink Feathers: Oksana Baiul"; *Storyscape Journal*: "At the End of Your Life," "Chandelier," "Communicant"; *100 Word Story*: "Rolling"

"Pussy Riot/Want/Don't/Want" appeared in *Nasty Women Poets: An Unapologetic Anthology of Subversive Verse* published by Lost Horse Press. "Napoleonic Series, 1974" appeared in *Plume Anthology of Poetry 2013*; "Fack You" appeared in *Plume Anthology of Poetry 3*; "Bare-Assed Hell" appeared in *Plume Anthology of Poetry 4*; "Vegreville Egg" and "Losing My First Language" appeared in *Plume Anthology of Poetry 5*; "Lord Taylor" appeared in *Plume Anthology of Poetry 6*; "Rolling" appeared in *100 Word Stories* anthology published by Outpost19 Books.

I am deeply indebted to Jay Hoffman for listening, for his encouragement and invaluable feedback on many of these poems. And, as always, my love and gratitude to the Orlowsky Hoffman Sestina Wright family, especially to you, Max, Raisa; Zoriah, Oliver (and others still finding their way). You, my family, are the greatest blessing in my life.

To Nancy Mitchell, godmother to my poems, for her remarkable insights and intuitive suggestions on many versions and drafts of this manuscript; to Jeff Friedman for his patience with my endless revision options, his humor, and for reading and commenting on many of these poems, particularly the prose poems; and to Gary Duehr for his final-hours help on some of the most stubborn poems.

I would also like to thank the following for their ongoing friendship and support: Kathleen Aguero, James Anderson, Genia Blum, Alan Britt, Barbara Siegel Carlson, Danielle DeTiberus, Melanie Drane, Lee Hope, Daniel Lawless, Gloria Mindock, Miriam O'Neal, Anne-Marie Oomen, Catherine Sasanov, Nicole Terez Dutton, Emily Van Duyne, Meg Kearney, Beth Grosart, Tanya Whiton—everyone in our Solstice MFA writing community of Pine Manor College.

Last but not least, a heartfelt thanks to Cynthia Lamb and Connie Amoroso for all your help on making this book happen. And my deepest gratitude to Gerald Costanzo for the pleasure and honor of working with you throughout the years and for believing in my work.

Book design by Kate Martin
Library of Congress Control Number 2018935064
ISBN 978-0-88748-638-8

Contents

Bad Harvest (A Sequence)

for Jay

*Even after a bad harvest,
there must be a sowing.*

—Seneca the Younger

Playing Opossum

My father carefully rolls his pant leg up, places his leg between
two wide boards. He tells my mother to jump hard on it.
Crippled, he won't be drafted. They agree. Earlier, he had
considered hiding under the living room's wooden floorboards,
but that would make him feel less of a man and more like an
opossum, paralyzed, blind. And weren't they known for their
short lives? Hadn't his friend Ihor, just the day before, avoided
enlistment by drinking a vial of his wife's blood, spewing it past
his cup of urine? Could he, too, do it: *drive a truck, heave honey,
blow grits*, trade his *rugged* for *ralph*, blow on his thumb until he
passed out? No, he was no greenhead looking for blood meal.
He had a wife, and they were in this together. She springs from
their horsehair-filled couch, eyes closed tight, fingers plugging
her ears; she lands with a thump. The leg doesn't break. He rolls
away from her, screaming, holds his hand up as if to strike the
air. Hysterical, she sobs through his curses. Forgiving her slight
body, he slowly closes his hand, lowers it over his heart.

Out of the Woods

Blood throbs against my uncle's eardrums as Nazis prod him
with rifle butts. His back grows wooden. When they leave,
he opens his eyes. Hell will find him, take a match to his soul,
blaze him into a human bonfire. He works his swollen tongue
into an oasis of melted snow, praying for rain. Saved from the
dead, gray mold of shallow graves, he turns over, lips quivering.
No soldiers emerging from the woods. *Someone is watching over
me*, each word, a rosary bead falling from his mouth. Above
him the blanched sky; but nowhere to be seen, the silver
branches of the watchful tree.

Mahogany Box

Lifting sealed ashes into flecks of sunlight, the funeral
director knows he's just performed a small miracle, turned
Baba into a well-made box my sister and I can drive home
in the front seat of her convertible VW Bug. In life, she was
never that easy. He asks if we're okay, the way we stare at it,
as if it were an undetonated bomb. He tilts the box to the left
then right, cautiously turns it in a complete circle. I imagine
a tiny trapeze artist inside spinning round and round from a
bar in the centre—white shirt, brown shorts, perfect calves in
white tights—sand trickling through the delicate apparatus.
At home, we move her around all the possibilities to a great
round of applause. She dangles, resting. We offer: shaded
among flowering wild onions or next to a vase on a bowed oak
mantel. *Is this the box you hoped for? No*, she answers. We carry
her downstairs to her basement apartment, encircle her with
wooden icons. They clear their throats in the dark.

The Fortieth Day

called forth a night of a different kind of brilliance when the
moon wrapped every thing with light—trumpeting yellow
pumpkin blossoms, a water pump with a dropped handle
resembling a rusty beard, an old chainsaw depression at the
top of a tree stump—things just outside her window that spoke
with feeble or hoarse voices. A minute passed . . . then another.
Old roses opened *fearless and beautiful on this day of sadness.*
Since, flowers were no longer just flowers, they blurred and
stretched into transparent curtains walking in the breeze of the
raised storm window, walking, for those of us left behind.

Napoleonic Series, 1974

A dozen black-inked prints of erections, ghost-fleshed and
silhouetted, each phallus prominently displaying an admiral
hat, too few to be called an army—their siege not *absolute*—just
quietly present in bright sunlight. How readily each took to
paper, cockades relinquished, their would-be nameless fame in
each signature bulk and roll. I could tell by the way Agnes, a
mid-forties conceptual artist, stared at me, her intern, that she
hoped her project would shock me all the way back to Ohio to
my split-level brick home off 10 acres of barren winter fields,
30 miles south of Cleveland. But I'd seen body transformed:
Cynthia Albritton's Plaster Casts, Jimi Hendrix's iconic hard-on,
Penis de Milo, fireproofed with dental alginate. It was a kind of
visual daring we lacked in our Midwest day-to-day. Assigned
to a corner of her studio, slouched over expensive graph paper,
I connected dot-to-dots of Agnes's 3-D model universe, listened
to the wash of street noise come in through her window,
careful not to disturb her deep mood. *This* was finally going to
get her into the Whitney Biennial. But it wasn't what you'd call
boner-worthy. Not like Hendrix's long fingers, kinky hair, black
Ultrasuede plumed hat and silver loops, air-humping his *Wild
Thing* Fender Strat, dropped to his knees, squirting lighter fluid
over Black Diamond strings, the world already on fire.

Electric Lady

My first day working the night shift at Electric Lady Studios switchboard was also my last. All I wanted was a chance to hang out with the musicians: on break when they would talk to me, ask me where I got my brown suede lace-up boots, or when I buzzed them in the back door to sign in. I'd be in charge of who comes in to lay down some tracks and who checks out for a quick smoke or to walk to the liquor store for a pint of Johnnie Walker. Maybe sit in on a recording session or two— there, right next to the soundboard. Party lines? Private Branch Exchanges? *No problem.* That first day, Johnny Winter was scheduled to come in. On my shift. Oh, hey. Yeah. *Was gonna rock like my back ain't got no bone. Was gonna roll like a wagon wheel . . .* Female jacks? Trunk lines? How hard could it be?

Lord Taylor

—after *The Colonel* by Carolyn Forché

What you've read on the coupons is true. An extra 20 percent off clearance items already marked 50 percent off, plus a one-time "just take it" pass if you use your black Premier card. I was new, there, at the fine jewelry counter. Just past security, the punch clock hung silent, hungry. Under counters, red rose logos loomed on folded white bags. *Shut up, say nothing.* There were daily sales reports, awards: *most-pleasant phone-voice*; *who-cashed-out-with-the-exact-change*; *who-leaned-on-the-glass-display-case-and-got-away-with-it*. There were security cameras. *Hello Hello* a sales woman cautiously called approaching a customer lingering in front of the faux pearls. We'd been trained to look for dressing room clothes swappers, duffle bag stuffers, thinking no one saw them. There was more: smile before swiping, swipe before refunding. Tactfully stifle gripes. First in English. Then in Spanish. *Cover for each other.* Today's specials were tired lace and linen tropical shirts, Tommy Bahama shorts cut just above the knees. I bagged the Cole Hahn "Water Under the Bridge" necklace in a lovely gold pouch, sealed it and passed it across the counter with a receipt to woman wearing a zebra printed coat. A wind came down from the escalator as she walked away, her drama stones clattering like glass. Adjusting his tie, leaning closer to me, Lord Taylor asked *how did it feel* making the first sale. He spilled out bags of gold hoop earrings. *Something for your commission, no?* Some of them fell silent. Discounted. Others seemed to come alive, listening, on the black cloth.

Chandelier

Birds sweep through gut strings of a forest. A tall, scarred
pine creaks in wind. Crows have long left their difficult nests,
long veins of green thorns knit with a dryer's screen scruff of
lint. They are done with late summer black masks, done with
waiting for the dust of earth to awaken; for those unwilling to
don down coats, join splintered winter roosts. Can you hear
them mocking our grassless yards? When it snows, streaks of
clouds drag color into my eyes. I lift my face to catch the flash
of ice breaking off our shingled roof, dirt-flecked prisms
melting into half sunlight before striking the ground.

Communicants

We know our sins by rote; they begin as part of a wide
unmarked road narrowing toward the front of the church
where, in that moment, I too eagerly lift my hands and the
priest holds back the wafer. He wants me to know, for that
moment, he's part of the road. *Not so greedily!* he hisses, but
loudly enough for the congregation to hear. Have I forgotten
to divulge every pilfered pencil and pocketed pen, bad thoughts
courted since childhood though they've changed, grown bigger
breasts and heavier balls? I cup one hand and place the other
on top. Forgiveness demands a throne—my atonement: wiping
down the refrigerator, scrubbing the toilet, bleaching my teeth
or sucking in my stomach. Behind me, my sister shuffles toward
the Eucharist like a 1960's Mr. Machine with see-through nuts
and bolts, head erect, tilted back. *These, my sins* her sluggish
main springs chug. After mass, the priest chuckles to himself,
hangs his gold vestment in the dark, dusty closet. He'll share
impressions with others—the *always something* we do wrong—
which, after coffee and Danish, he'll put his finger on.

Rolling

Late August, a black cat rolling in mown grass flips to its back
again, then rolls to its feet, half sun-drunk, half whiplash tail. I
am loved. Not. Am. I've mastered these tricks: At parties after
my husband's *break a leg*, rolling an ice cube on my tongue, my
eyes rolling over crowded rooms, my body buckled forward
rolling over rolling words. Rolling my eyes, having blood drawn,
the vial filling slowly as floodwater rising. Rolling through one
marriage then breaking it off, holing up, each of us rolling away
into our second marriages pretending, yes, to be dead.

At the End of Your Life

Elvis finally comes home for Christmas. You feel it in your
bones. But you're stuck with the Elvis impersonator who instead
appears every December for one night to entertain at Life Care
Nursing Home. Truth be told, you never really liked Elvis or his
hound dog, or the way he shook his leg like there was a mouse
shit-scared clinging to it that couldn't be knocked loose.

Elvis II believes it's the promise of *being blue without you* that
keeps the women's faces soft—not rotting-pumpkin-left-out-
in-rain soft, but *young lady* soft, stirred-from-dream-pulp soft.
He calls everyone *princess*, invites him or her to sing along, but
passes you—only you—the mike. You spit into it because that's
the way you kiss now.

Your children assume that each Christmas you're thinking
of them and how much money to leave each one, though
secretly you're thinking of Elvis's penis that like guava fruit
will be handed to you in the afterlife, sweet fleshed and spilling
its seeds.

You eat the neon-colored frosting cupcake the nurse's aid offers
to you, allow sugar to settle between your teeth. But this is not
you, not your style. Where is your pastel portrait drawn on black
construction paper, your hair wild as radish roots, eyes with
dark circles, as those on potatoes?

Before the set's over, your son hangs a complimentary strand of
violet Mardi Gras *Itzaparty* beads around your neck, ties to your
wheelchair a Mylar helium balloon that hereafter follows you
everywhere. *It's Bing Crosby who promises to come home, Ma—Bing.*
He offers to tuck you in an hour early.

But you curl back your lips, shake your head no. At the end of
your life, this is what love knows: someone always in a hurry
to go. Let them remember you as they will: a bargain basement
balloon; falling star-of-the-week; the last card you signed.

Fack You

Father called us into our room, sat on the edge of one twin
bed, head lowered, then lifting his eyes asked: *Have either of
you ever heard of the word . . . "fack?"* He pronounced it like he
pronounced "mashrooms"—immigrant doctor ordering pizza
at Fatbob's when Mother came up short on chicken livers
or tripe. He looked at us in disbelief, his now foul-mouthed
daughters. A houseguest had overheard us–me–scream *fuck!*
while driving the Ping Pong ball directly into the net, my sister
spinning wildly on her heels, her *ha ha's* booming up from the
dusky basement paneled with faux brick, a half case of 16-ounce
Cokes already chugged between us. We ached to be greaser
girls of teased hive hair, the runs in their black nylons an arrow
to their jutting hips as they slouched against the dumpster
smoking Lucky Strikes behind the pizza joint, a secret society
of popularity and sin, waiting for greaser boys to slink through,
slicked hair and black Banlon shirts, flipping the finger to
anyone who dared even walk past them—*Go fuck yourselves
you fuckin' motherfucker!*—Instead we were Father's two angels
carrying pails of water to a thirsty horse in our desiccated
meadow, no shade in sight—and Father, always running late,
making his rounds, dressed, always, in his Steve McQueen
sky-blue suit, revving his silver T-Bird roadster, later, the Hell's
Angel patient who came in for an allergy shot, catching him
instead napping on the gynecologist's table, his feet up in the
stirrups, an open can of 7 Up next to him. America had opened
its arms. But he had not done his job. At day's end, in the
parking lot surrounded by poppers pinging in shallow marshes,
in a moment of freedom, forgiven, we knew he'd put the blame
on the *pleased-with-herself* houseguest warming herself like
a fat August fly at our front window. *Fack her,* he'd whisper,
fumbling for his keys.

Given Plums

Early July my sister and I filled two sacks of plums from our orchard. We shook each tree until the ripest orbs fell from highest branches, closest to the sun. The less ripe ones hit hard as hail. The softer ones bruised or split against the recently mowed grass. Later we carried them to our neighbor who owned a 12-acre farm with sheep and one goat, 40 yards over. "Aren't these the best I ever had" he thanked us, pouring them into a large bowl. We hoped for more praise: Given how young and thin we were, and with such delicate hands—we shouldn't have gone to all the trouble. He offered back two of the plums for us to eat, but even though we waited there, he kept the empty sacks. Because he was a strong man with thick forearms flecked with golden hair who seemed to care about all things great and small, we imagined he used them to carefully gather the fruits of his hard labor or to sort his harvested crops. Instead, for the rest of summer, they drooped from a rusty nail in the corner of the barn. Earlier that day, Father had promised us two dollars for all the picking and gathering but later reneged on his offer. We remained empty-handed. He looked down at us from the porch. No rotting plums, no pits, and the grass now cleared for the next mowing. He smiled to himself like a man who had just made a dollar, like a man who just by looking past us could make it rain.

Vegreville Egg

Like a hornet caught in a jar, static buzzing between words,
he yells from across Manitoba's endless ice into the phone,
two provinces away from the world's second largest *pysanka,* a
Ukrainian-style Easter egg. Black-and-gold-tiled, it turns in the
wind like a colossal weather vane. Holding two separate rotary
phone extensions, my parents yell *It's Uncle Bohdan!* interrupting
each other in excited disbelief. Squatted on the floor next to
my mother's legs, I dress my naked Mary Poppins doll in spiked
heels and pretend also to be happy. Mathematically mastered,
steel-girdled, three-and-a-half stories high, weighing in at 2.5
tons—*we simply had to see it*—a pleasant 1,181-mile drive from
Ohio to Egg. We pack a picnic, boiled eggs and sardines. What
did we know about roadside burgers? But more pressingly, what
did we know of art? Except that our home—family and guests
insisted—aside from not having a framed print of the egg—was
filled with it: paintings *by our own kind* that *one day* my parents
whispered to us as if revealing an important family secret
would be worth a fortune—despite the fact that, it turns out,
these were not master oil paintings but rather, acrylic cartoons
of our people doing our-people kind of things—playing
Kitchkari, Ukrainian ring toss, or dancing in red leather boots,
multicolored satin ribbons streaming from flower wreaths in
women's hair, men sporting handlebar mustaches—paintings
that showed happy people, stomping and spinning in place.

Let the Dead Bury the Dead

Surely she would want to hear one final song, something from the Carpathians, something folkloric about flying geese or curly hair, just to calm her nerves before he laid her to rest. Or she might ask for a glass of chilled white wine, even though he never quite learned how to pour it well, forgetting to twist the bottle, or how to sip it, gazing into her eyes. He would have to find his domino cuff links, but first he would have to find his arms. He hadn't needed them for so long. The wind shushed through where his ribs once curled, a fat robin lodged itself in the invisible branches that spread where a human heart once beat. He'd remember not to wear his Adidas maroon three-stripe sweat suit, the one that made him sweat only if she saw him and grew angry. *This is not the way to seduce me,* her dark stormy eyes would reprimand. Should he bring a shovel? Could he bear to toss dirt on her remembering that he didn't particularly like it, the sound like heavy intermittent rain drumming on the roof of his casket, his friends staring into the burial vault, wondering what it would be like down there instead. Would she lie down quietly? He'd remember to reserve the moon. He'd ask a distracted God not to sweep too close to the stars. The tall grass would sway in the night breeze as if nothing had changed. Maybe he wouldn't need to bring his guitar, just his hands, if, he could remember where he last placed them. He hoped not to disappoint her with his cup of cracked black walnuts and a blushed apple unwrapped from a white lapel handkerchief, luring her into the next world. Any way, she was still very much alive. Night after night she stood in front of the bathroom mirror brushing back her filaments of fine hair. Why couldn't he see her there—spraying clouds of Paris Eau de Toilette in large continuous circles onto her white gauze nightgown, hear her reticent sigh.

Bare-Assed Hell

Those who lied or mocked hanged on a hook from their tongues over a fire; those who forgot to fast hanged by their bellies. . . . Devils poured hot tar down Father's throat for drinking and for hitting Mother. Baba licked the hot frying pan because of her backbiting tongue and for being a great sorceress . . .

—Alexander Dovzhenko, *The Enchanted Desna*

Punishment for misbehaving was not to be taken lightly, but when Mother condemned my sister and me to sit bare-assed on each other's bed pillows for fighting over the satin-trimmed comforter while watching *Beat the Clock*, we knew my family had arrived at another level of understanding: delivering an eye for an eye, or as Mother preferred, cheek for cheek.

She marched us toward our rooms. Along the deep sky-blue carpeted hallway separating us from crime and punishment, we imagined ancestors greeting us, tongueless and parched-throated, acknowledging us with sunken, sympathetic eyes, shrugging their shoulders as if to say, *told you so.*

My mother and sister entered my room first. Had I been allowed to follow them, I would've bartered for amnesty with a one of my night table's most sacred relics: a fluorescent green wooly Willy Worm coiled to strike or my mini cactus with an artificial flower straight-pinned into its side. Instead, Mother went directly for my pillow, squeezing it like an accordion; then, thumping it between her fists, she tossed it against the wooden headboard. *Sit!* she commanded. My sister whimpered as she climbed onto my bed, gingerly lowering her behind on my cotton threads.

Truth be told, I was concerned about the welfare of my behind. No matter how primly and properly we were raised, chances were that we both sweated and drooled in our sleep. On what, exactly, would I be sitting? I noticed that my sister's pillow had lost its fluff. It was lumpy and flat. I was sure condemned souls and devils smoldered there.

But what if we shared more than we dared to admit? We both loved pressing the down pillows against our faces, rubbing our lips back and forth against the warm freshly washed cases.

What if Mother, her kitchen timer set to 20 minutes, forgot about us while deadheading her roses?

She would come to my sister first. *First girl, best girl* would rise quickly to a tear-filled apology. Reluctant at first, Mother would withhold for a few seconds before finally releasing her from guilt. I imagined my sister pressing down a little extra hard against the sheets as she slid off my bed.

Free, my sister would want me still seated, exposed and vulnerable. We had become fixed features in each other's dreams. What was hers was now mine. What was mine had become hers. We were nothing more than asses—wider and heavier than storm clouds—more miserable than our ancestors who slurped cream or fried eggs with ham during fasts forced to sit, throughout eternity, bare-bottomed on hot frying pans.

Pleasure Pit

So she thoroughly taught him that one cannot take pleasure without giving pleasure, and that every gesture, every caress, every touch, every glance, every last bit of the body has its secret, which brings happiness to the person who knows how to wake it. She taught him that after a celebration of love the lovers should not part without admiring each other, without being conquered or having conquered, so that neither is bleak or glutted or has the bad feeling of being used or misused.

—Hermann Hesse, *Siddhartha*

That's basically how I remembered it—you know, having sex with Levi. Or as close as I thought I had come to having sex with Levi. I'd waited for months for him to drive up from Forest Hills having met him at a Ukrainian resort the previous summer. He played a Hummingbird acoustic guitar and sang with a melancholy voice, like he was at the end of his rope, hanging on for dear life. I fell for guys with voices like that.

In my parents' basement boiler room, a small space sectioned off with bamboo wall panels, we pressed our bodies together—our breaths punctuated by the occasional blast of the furnace. No one knew we were there.

Call it the fêng shui of hard attraction, you couldn't help it at seventeen: pull on a short chain, a ceiling lamp's red bulb lights and you're in sin city. Drop onto a mattress framed by wobbly scrap wood, and together you've found heaven. And this heaven had two amulets that hung voyeuristically above us: a cast iron hooked tail monkey and a carved one-eyed jack pirate coconut head.

But when I fell for Levi, I fell somewhere just slightly past fanned flames into *I don't love you* truth. The real truth when fake truth isn't paying attention. The kind of truth when the red bulb blows and the bamboo explodes in fire. And the upstairs toilet flushed sends water gurgling and swooshing through the pipes. Fifteen minutes of passion, and we were done.

Then he said it: *I'm so happy.*

In the pleasure pit, happiness was a dangerous intruder. It was a pair of sweaty socks. It was my Sweet Nothing pointy bra lying six feet from the laundry shoot and washing machine, fifteen feet from my father's vibrating belt exerciser and eighteen feet from our sauna formerly cold storage cellar where my grandmother skinned rabbits for pâté. In the pleasure pit, it was the soul's bad breath; it was Levi asking if there was a particular song I'd like to hear; the other voice that suddenly squeaks from a higher octave calling down: he's welcome to stay for dinner.

Why I Hate Nudist Camps

Wayne had already flung off his T-shirt, pulled off his black khakis to set up our tent—*I can work faster if I'm naked*—a new weed in the wet and wild. Faster, maybe, but not better: he slammed things together, tangled ropes. He was angry because we arrived too late to camp near the others. Because our Ford Country Squire was stuck in mud. Because I didn't bring the small shovel. Because that next morning he knew he'd have to get down on his knees, rake the mud away by hand instead of cannon-balling naked off the lake dock.

But there we were: In a light rain, surrounded by a scourge of mosquitoes; our pup tent's left hip sagging, missing a peg; the zip on, zip off flap—gone. I wanted to *call it a day*, a weekend, *I'm done!* and head back home to our triple-decker on Mission Hill.

What's the matter with you, Wayne barked as he sprayed repellent on his skin, careful to avoid his penis. What he meant was: why was I still wearing clothes—jeans and a hooded sweatshirt, a T-shirt and a pair of sunglasses—even though it was after five.

It wasn't because I imagined a couple of skeeters flying too low, curious about the new sweet sweat scent. Or because I had told him *Charlie's here*, and feared the absence of a tampon string would make me a liar. And certainly not because I'd feel inadequate or self-conscious around the other "campers" at the Get Down Hoe Down, pot bellies split with Caesarean scars, squash-shaped sagging breasts swaying joyfully, or that group sportin' softies at the Mister Softie Machine. No, I didn't give him the satisfaction. To hell, I thought.

The next evening, his chest slicked from dancing, he'd picked at his wrinkly steamed hot dog on his paper plate, looked out into the mob of flesh, and said *this* is where we belong. That he's not always going to look *this good*.

Babe, come on, he'd said, *take off your blouse. Just once get out of that busted radio of your mind always stuck on some high-strung wavelength.* The kind that always ruined the party.

Busted radio . . . *Okay Okay* I said, slowly pulling off my T-shirt.
Just enough skin to call it fixed.

He shook his head, *you really need to build up your shoulders.*

Bad Harvest

Even if it was mentioned, it was one sentence . . .

—*The Ukrainian Weekly*: "Day of Memory: Citizens
of Ukraine Share Recollections of Famines"

Swallow

Does my name take your tongue's
otherwise unclaimed space?

Swallow once for me.
These gooseberries are not stones,

this cup of water,
this cup of water.

500 Grams of Bread

My father worked, mother waited in line
at night for maloyem, crust thin as a wrist,
a breath, an octave

between one child
and the other lying in snow,
how blue that blue.

Dnister River Snails

faces, green gray,

like of those fallen with swollen bellies—

the snails promised
we'll hold you

until summer.

Eating Grass

no livestock   no chickens
no crumbs

hunger   if it could open its mouth wide enough
open its wide enough
open wide enough

hunger would tear
out the windows.

Shortly Before Deaths

of those already called back to air,

silk plums of your bruised feet split
& you dreamed, instead,

of slipping through any weightless surface.

Want

Come out we have a doll for you

neighbors disguised—kindly,
not succumbing.

Never open the door.

I am not afraid to speak of this

a cry from the heart
given by my parents,

a grain from the burning storage chamber
doused with kerosene,

the meat from the market—

no history
no pigweed, no stinging nettles left.

The Weakest of Children

What part of another's flesh
do you ask permission

for your body to be freed
from hunger the way

blood frees itself
from frozen earth,

in spring, when rain pours down
to wash everything.

Quietly a river refuses
to disappear into ground,

knowing it owes its mouth
to no one—

It runs instead
to the sea. How many words

need to be strung together
to be called history—

We promised to waste nothing,
thank whatever God understood.

How many of the weakest
do you try to call back—

so many rising
in the dark sky.

Invisible Departures

—internally displaced persons, Crimea, 2015

How long before choosing

to kiss an angel's hand,
to reach for heaven's

fruit-bearing boughs—
the bee not disturbed

too drunk—

How swollen the seeds
of heavy-headed sunflowers

that bow along the glass road
leading from home.

How silent the instrument
that comes down like a hammer

on someone leaving,
someplace left.

Inventory

A felt hat or a cane,
a pair of worn-out shoes

on a road thought
left behind—

or a hand-carved chess set
passed down from my grandfather:

the king's crown
a bent nail,

the knight's horse,
a nub on a pedestal

robbed of wings,
its would-be nose

blunt and chipped.
The queen can still fly anywhere.

Pawns are hardly worth her time:
Each quickly sacrificed

to vacant spaces,
each hoping instead

for a personal invitation,
for his own particular

key to sadness.

Stone Cross

—after Vasyl Stefanyk (1871-1936)
Ukrainian prose writer, political activist

1.

Remember your village of *always uphill*,
a water-warped leather neck strap,
the cramped wagon with an oak shaft.

Remember dirt, hunks of manure
flecked with feather and bone,
dust settled on the road before sunrise—

your horse hitched your nearside—
you, a saint, tied to a breast collar of rope,
forever carrying light on your back.

Bulging veins, engirded chains of blue steel,
your forehead swelled—
human sweat, animal sweat.

2.

If a thistle penetrates your foot—so what?

Blessed is that washed with saliva.
Blessed is the pinch of salt
buried in a wake of hooves.

3.

Remember it for its silence,

the hill where you staked
your life—stacked stones
into a cross, carved your name

into its old silt surface,
tiny phosphorous stars—

You knew no other marriage,
no other stony eyes.

4.

Cup your hands—
press them to your lips:

at times a deep-water wave uproots
a rock and washes it ashore, it remains
lying there heavy and inert.

From the rising and setting sun
it beholds the lively water and grieves that it no longer
bears its burden—

Losing My First Language

Ya mayu dornu minu:
I wear a stupid expression
and my sister agrees.

Gone my words for *pipe,* for
wig for *lovely daughter,*
for *may a duck kick you*

when someone presumed
dead shows up. Where
is the language of the nightingale,

of the child who received
the song of Ukraine when Saint
Nikolai ran out of toys?

Where are the words of barn
mice predicting bitter
winters, warning flood?

Ivan the Fly Eater

We could count on his appetite
for frantic

unexpected flights
or for accurate,

futile landings.
He caught flies the way some people

catch harsh words—
when least expected—

a slice of a lost argument,
the occasional punctuation mark filled with blood.

Rumors circulated that he also fed them to his cat—
unkind gossip

rampant as ugly old women.
Apologies fulfilled no purpose—

remorse was for rotting tree stumps.
We could count on Ivan

to lie complacently in the sun
near the wattle fence,

his face a welcome blank plate.
Besides, we had other things to worry about:

prystrit!, the evil eye, glaring solemn
curses at every turn:

May you choke on a bone!
May your son-in-law's legs shrivel!

Despite our gracious hearts,
sooner or later, we all suffered

under its weight.

Pussy Riot/Want/Don't/Want

I thought you were a catchphrase for the *not tonight, oh yes
tonight,* but not two nights in a row!
of late middle age

how else to say it:

*the thatched roofs are on fire
& the villagers have fled*

except this woman
whom you left behind,

her skirt rising in flames,
wild heat,

a wreckage of *K-Y* and Oil of Olay

* * *

O graying fraying housebound hive,
you're not my problem,

though I will admit

your spreading reflection in the handheld mirror
looks, this year—

don't make me say it—

wiser,

if not for love or song,

* * *

Can a finger dip into honey
in late January?

Can red wine stream like blood down my legs?

That afternoon, huddled against the cutting winter wind
in front of Boston's State House,

we protested

Putin must go!
Yanokovich is a cesspool!

while you, Prison punk prayer,
turn the world's attention
to

holy
hooliganism!

I thought you were a catchphrase for the want-don't want
of late middle age,

(oh pussy, what a riot, I had you all wrong)

Hope Was a Thing with Pink Feathers:
Oksana Baiul

Hope was a thing with pink feathers
circling Olympic ice.
Despite her tender years,
a woman of great composure.

Circling Olympic ice for gold,
Ukraine! We could hardly believe our ears:
This woman of great composure,
triple Lutz-flip-loop world premiere.

Ukraine! (We could hardly believe our ears)
representing the once orphaned and lost . . .
With a triple Lutz-flip-loop world premiere,
How much could one girl cost?

Representing the once orphaned and lost,
a dash of Broadway thrown in for good cheer.
How much could one girl cost?
Kerrigan, steely—no fame fetters yet or fear.

A little Broadway never hurt a routine—
Then: gold! Oksana cried and cried and cried.
Kerrigan gauged her steely dream:
It's taking twenty minutes for officials to find . . .

Oksana cried and cried and cried—let's say, triple-cried.
Post-Soviet tears no longer held to ransom.
It took twenty minutes for Olympic officials to find
Ukraine's national anthem.

As Nancy Kerrigan's eyes demanded ransom,
her Vera Wang swan about to be pronounced dead,
still no copy of Ukraine's national anthem—
maybe they'd play Russia's instead.

No flowers, swans or poppies red,
at home, we held our breath.
Maybe they'd fly Russia's eagle instead.
But damn, this gold was our destined wealth.

At home, we waited, held our breath.
Where was our anthem, the homeland tether?
Slava Boha . . . ! this could be our wealth.
Our hope was a thing with pink feathers.

Kalendar

sichen'—to slash

> Wind, do you use a scalpel
> so precise,
>
> it cleaves
> life-death's infinitesimal point,
>
> the soul released
> for its journey?
>
> ~

liutyi—fierce one

> And what, then, of the body?
>
> If only it, too,
> could fly away, never to return.
>
> The dead would stop worrying
> about coming back,
>
> sadly surprised to find
>
> hearts in puddles,
> faces in grass.
>
> ~

berezen'—birch tree

> Migratory birds
> carry God's blessings.
>
> But eyes watch other eyes
> for proof of love.
>
> ~

kviten'—blossoming of flowers

> Tsvetaeva was right—
> the body only gets in the way,
>
> Flowers rise as blood!

~

traven'—greening of grass

> Blade of grass, cut our lips—
>
> Tight between our thumbs
> we try to make you sing.

~

cherven'—larvae

> Earth line of black skeletal trees,
>
> what else besides gnawing
> have you forgotten?

~

lypen'—flowering linden tree

> A thousand years and still
>
> your music—
>
> praise of the lyre
>   or thud of drum
>
> naked
>   or prank?

~

serpen'—sickle harvests grain

> Smooth or serrated, tangled
> or burgeoning, dreams
>
> offer their undecipherable
> clusters of grains.

> ~

veresen'—ferns

> Our wooded
> > back acre is fluent
> > > in fern.
> *No silence,*
> *just phrases that can't be heard.*

> ~

zhovten'—yellowing of trees

> Press upon our lungs
> > to exhale—
>
> until fear streams
> > out of our spines, arteries,
>
> until we turn toward the color
> of one destiny.

> ~

lystopad—dropping of leaves

> Rain, the nervous wreck,
> > always tongues the always dark.

> ~

hruden'—frozen lumps of earth

Spring will terrify,
erupt from everything dead.

Apologetic
for lack of mountain range,

frozen lumps of snow and earth
no longer hold:

snih (snow)   to
     trava (grass)
       lybov (love)

Glue Wind

Elmer's Glue—swirled, rising into what her painter's eye
recognized as a pair of blowing snow funnels.
I had reassured her I saw them too, and pulling
her close said *Look, Tamara, if we squint,*
the tunnels shift slightly. And why is it
that, now, with her eleven years gone

I suddenly want to take it down from the wall,
as if to say once and for all: *glue is glue,*
others have done it. Though maybe not

with her 85-year-old arthritic hands. I could
put it somewhere between the pantry and crawl
space, cover it with a towel where it will pull

snow to it from an opened pack of flour,
until maybe, I'll uncover it again next winter.
Until then, in its place, I'll hang instead

her painting of violets. Not really
violets, after all, but more like a bouquet
of bruise-colored fingerprints. Where was it

I once read that German work camp
survivors often painted flowers?
Was it how they turned their minds away

from the dead—from eyes and skin
bleached by moonlight? I see her carefully
squeezing out several purple shades,

each one applied more thickly than the first,
wiping the excess with what looked
to be an old pair of her deceased

husband's briefs, the dark oils,
staining her fingers, her eyes straining
to see the flowers. Maybe,

even though I know it's just glue

and not the winter wind, every December
I'll return the painting back to its place

next to the kitchen window wall
where I can look at it while I eat, sip
warm tea: two funnels solidified

into something that, if I squint,
look like swirling snow—They could
be named anything.

Elegy

Black band of crickets,
shiny bodies, perfect anvil heads—
levitating above unmowed grass.

Their song passes through my window,
this breeze, hand-like, glove-like
fingers rubbing together,
searching for dust.

for W.L.

Names

Coughed into hands, scrawled
on damp surfaces, misspelled,
unrecognized, anesthetized,
analyzed. Our names tagged
as liars, out of control fires,
reinforced with wires, twisted
into barbs with pliers, claimed,
maimed—who put the blame on
the lame that spewed from us?
Before we fell in love. Before
What Ever Happened to Baby Jane?
happened to us, our hearts
crumbling like old mansions.
Before we signed off.

Purchasing Respirators at Home Depot
for My Family, Post-2016 Election

Mary Oliver's geese have stopped
heading home.
Symborska's white ants

have lost their signal.
William Stafford's river finally confesses
Hell if I know anymore . . .

Even the thickening sky can't keep
promises: wet paper tissues
and plastic grocery bags catch

on telephone poles, hatch
into dark lungs. Multipurpose
respirators, one size fits all,

instructions available in five languages.
I grab four: two for my husband and me;
one each for my son and daughter.

O face piece, filter cartridge,
chlorine and sarin gas,
asbestos, dust fumes, lead and lies—

making their way across the landscape,
announcing their place
in the family of things.

Fine Despite

Three days after my chemo infusion,
the hospital chapel's framed inspirational words
wishing us well in moving forward,
I send myself flying

with frozen lips and bad ski equipment,
arms and legs dragging
against the winter's cold molecules—
no longer regretting the frilly white gift

saved from the affair in Vaduz
that I wore during confession
under my street-length black
skirt, feeling its lusty long-ago

despite my diagnosis.
At the bottom of a hill
I stop as I started, stiff,
a few inches clear of a tiny pine tree.

I wish everyone could see me
sidestepping through woods.
I haven't felt so alive in years!
At least that's what you're supposed

to say when you've had cancer.
I don't want to let fellow club members down:
I'm riding shotgun with a shooting star.
I'm demanding my eighth-grade picture be retaken.

Half naked wearing platform shoes,
I slide down a greased pole.
Maybe that's what living means.
With a sympathetic priest looking on,

it used to be called dying.

Age of Osteo Collosus

Thank you doctor,
it must be so, each bone depleted—
each wish revealed.

Doll of fired clay & dried fruit,
of glassy-winged genitalia,
detritus of peanut brittle, cold

steel, pumice stone, partial
knee, rubble swan neck,
taxidermied hummingbird,

tumbling twigs, tumbleweed
joints, flared hand fans, ivory
splints, abridged bridge, thread-

bare spine, hips—exotic endangered
reefs, porous Taurus, X-Men, me.

Boston Burning: Mission Hill, 1984

in the lit-fuse voice
of the Environmental Protection Agency:
mind your own business—

the phone receiver slammed down
hard. My husband, naked as Ezra,
buckled in the corner, tearing out his hair.

PCB's reeking from subsidized housing,
dark smell, amber smell, mothball
smell. In fire ablaze on our balcony,

Now you've been warned—
altar of wood, bed of hot coals,
no cherubim saved, no angelic guardians,

no garland of laundry drying in night air.
Shadow scurrying in the dark.
In the Bromley-Heath Projects—no one

hurrying—*nothing here except*
roaches rushing out of a cooking pot.
In the Mission Hill auto parts shop,

the owner sitting vigil, shotgun at his side.
In a van pulled into the Heath Street Brewery,
two men rolling out tire after tire.

I've seen the wind carry fire.
In charred bricks, shattered glass,
foreclosed churches, vacant pews.

Fire, a witness of windows.
Fire, the night light.
Massachusetts Fire Academy,

red spilling across the sky.
Fire in the firehouse
dog's breath, lying.

Fire rising in stairwells,
Mayor Kevin White
stepping down—

Would we survive it,
the fire hungry fire—
in restaurants, in famished news,

in spit sizzling,
trees bristling,
in breath behind closed doors,

in houses sitting quiet?
Some doors take hours
to burn through,

others go in a flash—
Fire in the named and unnamed,
in notes of falling ashes.

⸝arate Bodies

It is an illusion that we are in separate bodies.

—Albert Einstein

Drug-punctuated veins, hands resting,
driving, not admitting to be tired,

we've taken on similar illnesses: sandbag face,
trees burning in each other's dreams.

You'd stand at the living room window
gazing out across a field

thinking how you loved to run, warm muscles,
cold showers, books kept under the bed,

saved for the one day they'd be read.
What are the questions we could've asked one another,

stirring words into small fires?
Leaning hard into the day, I still look

for you, drive to the water's edge
past November's vacant rooms, boarded windows,

my arms like branches wrapped
around the steering wheel.

I was always listening, always there.
I've stopped listening.

But tell me there is more
than the color of our eyes.

for my father

Folding a Stranger's Laundry

You didn't tuck a quick love note
into the front pocket of his denim Levis shirt
or begin to sing "Teach Me Tonight" under your breath,
two years and counting after your divorce.
Instead you hung around the dryer pretending
to have accidentally dropped one
of what no doubt had to be
a favorite pair of socks,
the one that would suddenly appear,
a stowaway hitched onto an oversized towel,
a turn of luck, a good omen.

You didn't find a woman's slippery
nightgown among his workout gear,
a citrus-colored thong for you
to peel slowly apart from his Under Armour,
dismissing the sparks. You didn't
have to say a prayer for love to find you,
then and there, in a basement laundry room.
Prayers, you believed, were meant for bigger
things—for, as a child, remembering to sleep
with your hands above your blankets,
luminous rosary beads
woven between your fingers.

You only had to lightly tug on his torn T-shirt
for it to tumble freely out of the drum,
to imagine it, instead, as a favorite rag
with which he wiped down a saxophone,
playing a few licks and phrases,
after sunset, in his soundproofed bedroom,
his pants, flecked with white paint,
from perhaps painting a fence. For once,
you didn't have to reinvent yourself
in the lint-colored light, the bare bulbs
and giveaway magazines,
swab your lips Sax Saver red
then slip into a shiny metallic
crop top and jeans.

You just had to be there, then,
that afternoon—
no one around,
his laundry, done,
except for one last shirt you left unfolded,
sky blue,
it seemed,
opening its arms to you.

for Jay

NOTES

The epigraph to "Bare-Assed Hell" is my translation from the original Ukrainian.

In "The Weakest from Children," the lines: "We promised to waste nothing, thank whatever God understood" are quoted from the poem "Every Decision" by Robin Hamilton.

In "Stone Cross" the last two stanzas are quoted from Stefanyk, translated by Anatole Bilenko.

My title "Hope Was a Thing with Pink Feathers: Oksana Baiul," is a variation on Emily Dickinson's "Hope Is the Thing with Feathers."

In "Kalendar" the lines "No silence, / just phrases that can't be heard" are quoted with slight variation from Alejandra Pizarnik's poem "Being" translated by Yvette Siegert. And the lines *snih* (snow) / *trava* (grass) / *lybov* (love) are quoted with slight variation from Askold Melnyczuk's poem "And So." Subtitles correspond to Ukranian months of the year.

In "Purchasing Respirators at Home Depot for My Family, Post-2016 Election," the lines: "making their way across the landscape / announcing their place / in the family of things" are quoted with slight variation from "Wild Geese" by Mary Oliver.